Swimming Lessons: The Best Lessons Explained

Miriam F.

Contents

Furthermore, the information that can be found within the pages described forthwith shall be considered both accurate and truthful when it comes to the recounting of facts. As such, any use, correct or incorrect, of the provided information will render the Publisher free of responsibility as to the actions taken outside of their direct purview. Regardless, there are zero scenarios where the original author or the Publisher can be deemed liable in any fashion for any damages or hardships that may result from any of the information discussed herein.

Additionally, the information in the following pages is intended only for informational purposes and should thus be thought of as universal. As befitting its nature, it is presented without assurance regarding its prolonged validity or interim quality. Trademarks that are mentioned are done without written consent and can in no way be considered an endorsement from the trademark holder.

INTRODUCTION

Swimming is the practice or operation of using your muscles to move yourself through the mud.Swimming can be an individual sport, or a team sport.

There are different forms of swimming including breaststroke, freestyle, backstroke, and butterfly.

Swimming is for all, no matter what age or fitness level. Any age can learn to swim and when you can't swim there's no age limit. Swimming is a natural talent that can save your life or that of another. Appended to dive is never too late. Staying fit can be achieved as a result of swimming with most swimming baths are suitable for everyone. Single woman, parent and child, senior groups among others

A swim suit is all you need to get going. You can also ware up swimming tops or close fitting t-shirts until you feel better. We'd also recommend sunglasses to protect your eyes.

The nice thing about swimming is it's a relatively low-maintenance, low-cost exercise to take on. Unlike other sports such as swimming, rock climbing, or even running.

Goggles and suits come in all shapes, colors and sizes. Ultimately you may want to invest in devices such as a pull buoy and paddles, or Zoomer fins to complement your exercises and add variety.

First, find a local swimming pool with reasonable lap hours, and agree to two or three weekly visits. You really need to find time for at least twice a week, or the growth and relaxation will be painfully slow in the pool.

Absolute beginners, either group or adult, should ask about the lessons. Group lessons may be better but you can find private lessons for a bargain if you are resourceful enough to make any inquiries.

Try to ask the local pool if there are lifeguards willing to give 30-minute lessons on their day off, or if there's a squad of high school swimmers searching for some extra pocket money of leaders. Most teens in swimming classes will jump at the chance to earn extra money this way (it beats mowing the lawn), and an average of $20 a half-hour lesson is a bargain compared to private swimming coaches in fitness and country clubs that charge you an hour.

If you can afford these lessons, they can be very helpful and inspiring, but it's always wise to search around for a low-cost option. For sporting magazines the Web and online advertising are also ways to find information.

If you're completely unaccustomed to the water and are scared even to get your face wet, you might want to try aqua-aerobics as a way to get going in the shower. Hugely popular among seniors and weight-loss applicants who have no sporting experience, this is a low-impact, non-intimidating sport that's a perfect way to overcome any discomfort you might have as a newcomer in the pool. A lot of native clubs pools usually have scheduled aqua-aerobics lessons, so ask if you are interested.

If you have some exposure of swimming (i.e. you can float and maybe do a few laps), a nearby masters program can be a great athletic and social opportunity for you. It is an orchestrated routine normally conducted by a professional instructor who can provide support and advice in preparation. You're going to share a lane with several others and do mostly interval training so you can have a different pool experience than you're used to doing.

Finally, swimming in the pool involves a certain amount of skill and knowledge in the basic reading of clocks and the calculation of metric distances

CHAPTER ONE

BENEFITS OF SWIMMING

Swimming is a great training because you need to move your whole body against water resistance.

Swimming is an excellent overall activity for the following reasons:

1. Is suitable for people with disabilities, arthritis, and other conditions Swimming can be a healthy fitness option for people with:

- Arthritis
- Accident
- Disability

- Other Issues that make high-impact swimming workouts painful may even help to reduce some of the discomfort or enhance the healing from injury.

One study showed that people with osteoarthritis registered significant reductions in joint pain and stiffness, and felt reduced physical limitations when engaging in activities such as swimming and biking.

Even more concerning, the advantages between the two classes ranged little to no overlap. Therefore, it seems that swimming has many of the same advantages as commonly recommended land activities.

2. Great option for people with asthma: The warm indoor pool environment makes swimming a perfect sport for asthma sufferers. Not only that, but sport-related breathing exercises, like holding your breath, will help you increase strength in your lungs and enjoy a more controlled breathing.

Some studies suggest swimming may increase your risk of asthma due to the chemicals that are used as treatments for pools. Consult your doctor about prospective swimming hazards if you have asthma, and try out a pool that contains salt water instead of chlorine if possible.

3. Beneficial for people with MS, also people with multiple sclerosis (MS) may find it beneficial to swim. Water makes the limbs buoyant and helps them support during exercise. Water gives a soft resistance, too.

A 20-week swimming regimen resulted in significant pain reduction for patients with MS in one study. Those participants also reported changes in symptoms such as exhaustion, depression and impairment.

4. Swimming Torches calories is an effective way of burning calories. A 160-pound individual burns about 423 calories an hour while swimming laps at a low or moderate pace. That same person could burn up to 715 calories an hour swimming at a faster pace. A person of 200 pounds doing the same exercise will burn between 528 and 892 calories an hour. Somewhere between 632 and 1,068 a 240-pound person could burn.

When equate those figures with other common low-impact sports, the same 160-pound person would only consume about 314 calories walking for 60 minutes at 3.5 miles per hour. Yoga could burn only 183 calories an hour. And in that hour the elliptical machine could be eating only 365 calories.

5. Enhances your sleep: Swimming may have the influence to facilitate your night's sleep. In an insomnia research of the older adults, following routine aerobic exercise, participants reported both an improvement in quality of life and sleep.

Up to 50 percent of older people suffer a degree of insomnia, so this is great news. The study focused on all aerobic exercise types including elliptical, stairmaster, bicycle, pool, and video exercise.

Swimming is open to alot of people dealing with physical problems which make other exercises less appealing, such as running. That may make swimming a good choice for older adults looking to make their sleep better.

6. Boosts the mood Scientists tested a small group of dementia patients and saw mood change when engaging in an underwater 12-week program. Swimming and water workouts are not just psychologically beneficial for dementia sufferers. Exercise has been shown to improve many people's attitude, too.

7. Helps manage stress: Instantly before and after swimming at a YMCA in New Taipei City, Taiwan, researchers tested a group of swimmers Of the 101 individuals surveyed, 44 reported being slightly depressed and experiencing stress

associated with fast-paced life. The percentage of people who continue to report feeling overwhelmed after swimming decreased to just eight.

While more research is needed in this field, the researchers conclude that swimming is a potentially powerful means of rapidly relieving stress.

8. Secure during pregnancy Apart from bathing, pregnant women and their babies can also enjoy some great rewards. In one animal study a swimming of a mother rat was shown to alter the development of the brain in her offspring. It may even shield babies from a form of neurological issue called hypoxia-ischemia, but it requires further research. In addition to potential benefits for the child, swimming is an activity that can be carried out in all three trimesters.

Another study shows no side effects of swimming during pregnancy in chlorinated pools. Early and mid-pregnancy pregnant women who swam reportedly had a reduced risk of premature labor and congenital deficiencies

Keep in mind that while swimming is generally considered safe during pregnancy, many females may have movement limits due to complications of pregnancy. Check with your doctor before starting your new workout routines breastfeeding, and inquire for healthy exercises if you are having complications.

9. Good for kids too Children need at least 60 minutes of aerobic exercise every day. It also need not feel like a burden. Swimming is a fun activity and does not necessarily feel like working out in a formal way.

You can either do structured swimming lessons or be part of a swimming team. Another good way to get children going is unstructured pool time.

10. Additionally, inexpensive swimming can be an economical fitness option compared to others, such as cycling. Many pools offer reasonable admission rates. Many public schools and other facilities offer free swimming hours, or a sliding scale based on your salary.

More benefits includes:

- Continues to increase heart rate, but removes some of the impact stress from the body
- Build endurance, strength and cardiovascular fitness
- Helps in ensuring a healthy weight, heart and healthy lungs
- Tones muscle and builds strength

- It provides full-body exercise because almost all muscles are used during swimming.
- Relaxed and calm exercise
- Reduce stress
- Improve coordination, balance and posture
- Increased flexibility
- Provide low-impact therapy for some injuries and symptoms
- Provide a comfortable way to cool on a hot day
- Free in many locations – bathing in swimming pools, beaches, reservoirs, rivers and streams. Make sure you pick the right and safe environment to swim in.

FEAR OF SWIMMING

Most of us have a degree of concern when it comes to water. Normally, we're going to overcome these fears or find ways to deal with them. But if you have aquaphobia or fear of water, you suffer with a constant and uncommon amount of fear and anxiety that keeps you from going close to water.

Aquaphobia is a special phobia. This is an unreasonable fear of anything which doesn't exist and which gives rise to much risk. You may have aquaphobia because you feel that any water source gives you an unhealthy amount of anxiety. This may include a swimming pool, a lake, an ocean, or even a bathtub.

Aquaphobia is sometimes misunderstood for another phobia ,hypophobia. Although they both contain water, aquaphobia and hydrophobia are not the same thing.

Hydrophobia is a water aversion that occurs in humans during the later stages of rabies.

The National Institute of Mental Health reports that 19.2 million people in the United States are affected by different phobies. Girls are twice as likely to encounter them as males.

Some people who have a particular phobia, such as aquaphobia, are starting to develop symptoms related to their anxiety of infancy or puberty.

Seeing water can cause intense fear and anxiety in an aquaphobic person. That could be very low water, such as what is found in the bathroom sink, or a huge body of water, such as the ocean. The amount of water is not what causes phobia. It is the water itself that gives rise to fear and to the resulting anxiety.

Some of the most common symptoms of aquaphobia include: an immediate feeling of intense fear, apprehension, and discomfort when talking of water, constant, excessive, or unnecessary fear when exposed to water, realizing that the fear of water is unreasonable or out of proportion to the actual threat to stop water sweating fast heartbeat close to the chest, and difficulty breathing nausea or dizziness.

The origins of common phobies are not well known. Nevertheless, there is some suggestion that phobias can be transmitted biologically. If you have a member of your family who has a mental health issue, like paranoia or other phobia, you can be at risk of suffering a phobia.

Aquaphobia is sometimes the result of a traumatic childhood event, such as near-drowning. It could also be the result of a series of negative experiences. These usually happen in adolescence and are not as serious as a traumatic experience.

It is also proposed that changes in brain activity may also play a role in the development of different phobias.

Physicians are using the new edition of the Diagnostic and Statistical Manual of Mental Disorders (DSM-5) to help them treat mental health conditions.

Currently, the DSM-5 does not have a specific diagnosis or aquaphobia type. Alternatively, it describes the fear of water as part of a common phobia disorder.

When you think that you have aquaphobia, make an appointment with your doctor. We will be able to refer you to a mental health specialist who can diagnose and treat your phobia.

Based on the criteria of the DSM-5, a mental health practitioner is likely to treat aquaphobia (or a similar phobia) if you have endured the above symptoms for at least six months.

Part of the treatment also requires the removal of other mental health conditions, such as obsessive-compulsive post-traumatic stress disorder panic disorder.

Because aquaphobia is considered a particular phobia, it is most frequently treated with two types of psychotherapy: relaxation therapy and cognitive behavioral therapy.

Exposure therapy is the standard method of treatment. You will be repeatedly exposed to the root of phobia — in this situation, water — during this type of therapy. As you are exposed to water, the doctor can keep track of your responses, emotions, perceptions, and experiences and help you manage your anxiety.

Through cognitive behavioral therapy, you can come to doubt your thoughts and beliefs about your fear of water. When you learn to confront your assumptions, you will also build strategies to deal with these patterns of thought and perception.

To addition to professional treatment, there are also a variety of self-care strategies that you can use at home. Mindfulness-based approaches, daily physical exercise, meditation, and deep breathing are all effective techniques for overcoming phobias.

During later stages of therapy, you can decide to work with a specially trained swim coach who can help you learn how to feel comfortable swimming.

TIPS TO OVERCOME THE FEAR OF SWIMMING

It can be hard to overcome the terror of swimming. It can keep a lot of good people back off from learning to swim, but it does not have to be that way. Many pools offer beginner lessons in a friendly and welcoming setting, and you'll meet a lot of people who have the same background as you.

A few tips to help conquer the fear of swimming

Start by getting your feet wet and try to slowly get deeper into the pool When you can stand far enough in the water to spray water on your face as if you were brushing it.

Think of positive images at the same time as you splash your face.

First, try to learn how to hold your breath under the surface and breathe out into the cold. Blow the bubbles, essentially!

Keep your hand and exercise kicking your body stretched out Don't feel hurried to make progress.

So then, note that you're not alone.

SAFETY SWIMMING RULES

Always swim with friends.

Swim only where the guards are.

Avoid water when you are very tired, very cold, or overheated.

Follow all swimming rules posted in the swimming area.

Follow Lifeguard's instructions.

If you cannot see the bottom of the pool at the deep edge, or if the water is cloudy, do not swim.

Avoid swimming in unlit areas at night.

Do not chew or eat gum while swimming. There is a possibility of suffocation.

Do not push, push or run near water. Playing with horses is dangerous.

If you hear or hear thunder, get out of the water.

Swim a safe distance from diving boards and slides. Never swim under them.

Never swim near the slopes of dams or boats.

Avoid swimming in the river.

POOL SLIDE RULES

The slide must be deep inside the pool. This allows water to enter more than 8 feet away from the diving area.

Lower your legs first in a sitting position. (Going down from your head is dangerous; it can hurt your head, neck, or back.)

BEACH RULES

Know where the nearest lifeguard stand is.

Be sure to check your surfing before entering the water.

Check the warning flags.

Watch for signs of danger.

Swim well away from piers, piles and diving platforms.

Beware of dangerous marine life

Remember that if you swim from the shore, you have to swim back.

If you are caught in a tide, do not fight or swim. From there you can gradually swim back to the shore.

Do not put pressure on dangerous stunts.

Water park slides, waterways, wave pool rules

Check that there are observers in all areas.

Before you begin, determine your position carefully.

Do not put pressure on the stunt.

In the wave pool, be sure to check how deep the water gets when you turn on the wave pool.

CHAPTER TWO

SWIMMING SCIENCE

Human beings formed from sea creatures but you would never guess it— looking at our bodies. If we tried, we couldn't be any less suited to traveling across mud. We don't float too well, we can't breathe long under the surface and we quickly tire as we maul through the water attempting to move along; you'll still come last with a dolphin or a shark in a direct race! But we humans do have one big advantage: we know about science.

We understand how forces work to our advantage, and how to use them. If you have never thought of swimming as a science, the time to start is now. Apply some scientific thinking and you will find that you can swim far more efficiently. If you're a nervous nonswimmer, you can give you enough confidence to break through your fear by thinking about the solid science which keeps people afloat. What are we asking for, then? Let's take a dip — with a closer look at water education!

Swimming pushes the body through water (a highly viscous fluid) that is either calm (as in a pool), turbulent (as in the ocean), or somewhere in between. If you're floating entirely beneath the surface (scuba diving, for example), you're passing across fairly calm water; other times, you're going to move along at the more fluid intersection of air and water, with your hands, limbs, head and body shifting from one dimension to another and back again, speeding up or slowing down as they cross the border.

WATER VS AIR

Before we can comprehend aquatic physics, it helps to know that air (a gas) is very specific from water (a liquid). The primary difference is that water is considerably denser (the same amount weighs much more) and viscous (i.e., thicker—similarly, treacle is more viscous than wine).

Air and water variability makes a huge difference to how we can travel on air and land. When you're walking on land, the main thing is to work against gravity which your body should help you out with (lifting your legs, swinging your arms, and keeping you from overturning through constant balance adjustments) and a bit of friction where your shoes meet the ground. If you move faster (say, on a bicycle), air resistance becomes a force that is more important than gravity; unless you walk into a really strong wind, you barely notice the air while you walk. When you're in the sea, gravity is far less important because it's effectively canceled out by your buoyance (tendency to float). As a swimmer, the main force you have to worry about is drag water resistance. We are going to get to that in a second.

When you swim outdoors, especially in the winter months, certain variations between water and air are important: since water is much denser than air (more specifically because it contains many more molecules per unit of volume and these molecules are bound together), it absorbs heat of your body around 25-40 times quicker than air at about equivalent temperature. (That is why swimmers and "wild" open air swimmers usually wear wetsuits to prevent hypothermia, a very harmful cooling of the body's core that can murder you.), it takes a lot longer to warm up. That's why the ocean temperature typically lags 2–3 months behind the earth temperature in countries like the United States ' East Coast and the United Kingdom (where the ocean is often warmest in September).

NEWTON'S SWIMMING LAWS

If you enjoy science but you're terrified of water, you'll find it very helpful— as I did as I learned to swim — to talk about the three laws of Newton's motion. These three basic principles are sufficient among the most fundamental rules of physics to fully explain the movement of nearly every single object you're ever likely to come across.

The first law sets out the concept of resistance. It says things stay still or move steadily (at the same speed) unless they are pushed or pulled by something (unless some form of force is applied). The latter and third principles are of greater interest. The second law describes the relation between force and acceleration: if you move or pull it, it continues moving (if it was still to begin) or it goes faster (if it was already moving); the greater the force you apply, the greater the acceleration you get; the longer you apply the force, the greater the velocity change you will produce.

The third legislation is perhaps the most important when it comes to swimming. It says the object returns the favor when you apply a force to an object, and applies you an equal force — in the opposite direction. This rule is often called behavior and response and a practical non-swimmer has the best way to make use of the surface. You probably already know that if you kick back against a swimming pool bank, you're flying through the water sideways. The same holds true with real swimming strokes. Simply speaking, you have to pull water backwards with your hands if you want to swim forward through the water. If you desire your body to be kept up and float on the surface you need to kick your legs down. If you're swimming along and want to stop and stand up suddenly, you can pull your hands down in front of you (in a type of round motion— somewhat like bowing down) and your legs will swing behind you, so that you'll land upright on your feet. Master these basic moves— simple applications of the third law of Newton— and you'll find you can swim easily and stop with confidence whenever you need to.

MINIMIZING YOUR DRAG

Minimizing your drag will make a big difference to how well you can move through the water. Once you have mastered the basic science of swimming, the next step is to minimize your drag in the water: that will help you swim more quickly and for longer, using the minimum amount of energy in the process. This is not always known by many beginners, but it's just the same as cycling: just as riders have to reduce the surface area they pose to the wind (crouch down, bring their arms under, and basically streamline themselves), so swimmers have to generate as little water resistance as they can. In reality, this includes making your body literally horizontal, so your head is well down in the water (in the case of the front crawl) instead of picking up with your body overhanging behind it. (That's why you've got to learn to exhale in and breathe out underwater.) You can also reduce friction by slicing your hand in and out of the water to make your movements, and you can learn to move (rotate) your body from side to side when swimming. And it helps rotate your knees so point your toes like a ballerina, so that your feet don't sink like tires in the mud.

It is worth noting that, for several reasons, sea-water is harder to swim in than pool-water. First, the ocean is sometimes more turbulent, except on magnificently calm summer days, so your body isn't like a dolphin drifting through the water. Also, seawater is denser than freshwater due to the extreme salt it comprises and that makes it a bit more viscous too. Yet cold water is more viscous (in the ocean) than hot water (in a heated pool); water viscosity at 10 ° C (50 ° F) is at 40 ° C (~100 ° F) twice that of water. All these things make swimming a cold ocean a tougher prospect than bathing in the heated pool, but the upshot is that the body works better and gets more workout.

Unlike cycling or sprinting through the air, when you're swimming it's hard to build up any momentum: although you're sure to glide for a short time, water resistance will still get you to a halt quickly. What we've got here is first motion law in action. If water were as light as air, but you could still float and swim through it, you could stroke and rest for a while, allowing your momentum to keep you moving forward (as often as you can stop pedaling on a bike). But the water's force pushing against you is quick to bring you to a rest. When you try to change direction, you will also experience inertia: since velocity is speed in a particular direction, changing direction means changing velocity— and it requires you to use a force, even if you swim at constant speed. If you're walking at the front and you decide that you want to turn around in a semi-circle and go back the way you came, it's really hard to change the direction of your travel without halting and turning or doing a sunsault.

Swimming effectively is superb aerobic exercise (vigorous exercise that really pumps your heart and lungs) and very tiring; of course the two things are connected. By swimming more efficiently you can swim further for longer, which implies using it as little energy as possible for each stroke by reducing drag, and gaining as much forward thrusters as you can.

The object is to broaden your hand as far as you can with front crawl and drag it back as much as possible, trying to drag as much water back (with a cupped hand and a bent forearm) as you could possibly. (Swimming teachers call this two-part process a "catch" and a "pull.") If you do a long, complete stroke with proper follow-through, you apply your pulling force longer and each stroke counts for more. You also see this from the second law of Newton's motion, that is often written: force= mass= acceleration F= m a Because acceleration is velocity divided by time, it's also true that force is proportional to the rate of momentum shift: F= mv / t and that: force= time= mass= velocity F t= m v To put it another way, if you want to make the biggest possible momentum change, you need to force yo It is also worth remembering that the human body is a machine (in the strict scientific sense of that word): our limbs operate like levers, pivoting at our joints (which are effectively fulcrums), multiplying force or speed. When you're crawling at the front, it's necessary to pull your arm back as far as you can. That way, you get more control on the water and the energy you generate to pull backwards allows you more power to go forward. A successful follow-through often decelerates the arms more gradually, and decreasing the force decreases the strength they experience, thus reducing the likelihood of pulled muscles and other injuries.

Conserving momentum tells us that your body's momentum, going forward, is the same as the momentum you give the water, pulling backward. Which means you have to pull back as much water as you can with each stroke. Cutting your wrist helps; holding your elbow straight when you pull back helps too, and your forearm acts like a raft, so you pull back all the water worth of your limb instead of just a fraction. You will find that to start with, this is much harder and more tiring, which is a good sign: it shows that you are creating much more force.

Energy and power Pushing your body through the water takes energy — and your body loses the same amount of energy in the process. The rate at which energy is used for something is called power. Champion swimmers can achieve a power of 1200 watts briefly (the maximum power of a washing machine for clothes or a very powerful vacuum cleaner), similar to what a champion cyclist can achieve for short periods of time, pumping away flat. The swimming power figures which are in the hundreds of watts. This is compatible with the strength that top cyclists regularly produce Moving and buoyancy Objects float because when we position them in water, the water pressure under them forces them up and helps them; in other words, water pressure pushing up equilibrium weight (gravity force) pulling downward. That's one of the reasons we're swimming in a horizontal position: spreading the flat body makes it work more like a raft, so there's more uptrust from below water. You probably know that floating on your back is much easier than standing upright when you need to "travel water" (kick and push down your arms to create an upward force that will stop you sinking).

The biggest fear of a non-swimmer is slipping under the water and dying, but sinking is much easier than you might imagine when you are swimming. (Apart from when you suddenly fall into a pool, where you are more probable to sink and drown because your clothes get soaked because you avoid swimming properly; conditions such as water temperature also play a part.)

Based on your body type (how big you are, how often you weigh, how big your lungs are, how overweight you are, and so on), you might be incredibly amazing: you might find it very challenging. It is pretty well known that overweight people are more permeable than skinnier people and this is because fat is less dense (more buoyant) than muscle. Choosing to wear a wetsuit (made from a synthetic rubber called neoprene that soaks up air bubbles inside it) allows you even more buoyant, which is why scuba divers generally have to carry weights to help them sink.

Is floating better, or sinking better? If you're a boat, do one or the other of course is better! Unfortunately, most boats are doing a bit of both: crashing and dragging straight through the waves— in the very turbulent interface between air and water. The fastest boats are hovercraft and hydrofoils (which aim to lift themselves off the waves) and submarines (which sink under them). If you're a swimmer, then none of these is an option. We can't choose to sink or float: we need to pull in the mud. Even so, understanding the science of swimming and learning how we apply it can help us poor soil creatures pass through the water as efficiently as possible!

SWIMMING HYGIENE

Healthy swimming behaviors: Although chlorine and other disinfectants are an excellent way of killing germs present in drinking water, they do not work immediately.

Given the use of disinfectants, many people have become ill with aquatic water infections (RWIs), caused by germs transmitted by coughing, breathing in mists or aerosols from swimming pools, hot tubs / spas, lakes, dams, or oceans. RWIs include infections with the gastrointestinal tract, skin, hair, respiratory tract, leg, neurology and burn. Diarrhea is the most commonly reported RWI, caused by germs including Cryptosporidium ("Crypto"), and E. Colleli 0157:H7.

Over the last two decades the number of RWI outbreaks has grown. Know chlorine and other disinfectants do not immediately kill germs. For fact, adding bleach with urine and saliva requires chlorine in the shower, otherwise it would kill germs.

We all share the water in which we swim and each of us needs to do our part to help keep us, our families and friends healthy. By learning more about Swimmer Protection you can help prevent the spread of germs which cause RWIs.

To help protect yourself and other swimmers from germs, all swimmers should take a few easy and effective precautions while we swim: keep the piss, vomit, sweat and dirt out of the pool!

If you have diarrhea stay out of the water.

Shower before going into the shower.

Don't piss in the tub, or vomit.

Don't spill the cold.

Any hour— all out!

Take the children out on breaks in the shower.

To keep germs away from the pool, check the diapers and change them in a toilet or diaper-changing area–not poolside.

Apply sunscreen over again.

Drink lots of fluids.

Check the level and pH of free chlorine before going into the bath.

Pools: Proper free levels of chlorine (1–3 mg / L or parts per million[ppm]) and pH (7.2–7.8) maximize germ-killing.

Hot tubs / spas: Correct amounts of disinfectants (chlorine[2–4 parts per million or ppm] or bromine[4–6 ppm] and pH[7.2–7.8]) improve the ability to kill germs.

Many pharmacies, hardware stores, and pool supply stores sell test strips from pool.

SWIMMING AIDS

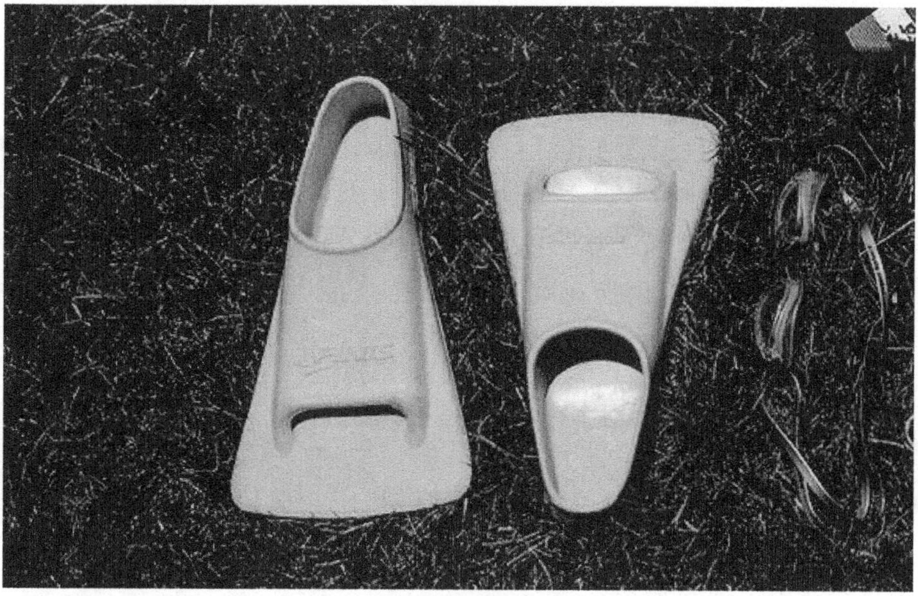

SWIMMING GEAR FOR BEGINNERS

Let's make sure you are covered with all the basics to get your swim workouts started.

Step 1? Buy good bathing suit! You can go with a one-piece or two-piece for water exercise, though the one-piece has some definite benefits. If you are going to do a lot of laps, a one-piece is best because it allows your shoulders to move freely and when you dive into the water they won't fall down or slip off.

For paddle boarding or other activities in the pool, two-piece suits can be perfect, but because they aren't as sleek as one-piece, they aren't the safest for lap bathing. Suits are supposed to fit well but not too heavy. If the straps bite into your neck, or because some pain, go wider. Based on your needs many of the items listed below are available.

Swimming fins are a great tool to use while you are learning the fundamentals because they increase your kicking ability. And, while you use them, you can concentrate on your arm movements and your breathing.

When you're underwater a good pair of goggles can help protect your eyes. When you regularly wear glasses or contacts, and swim, you may want to find a pair of prescription goggles.

Swimming caps are a must for casual swimmers, if chlorine is to cover the scalp. You want one that's snug and stays up while you're swimming. You won't keep your hair 100 percent dry, contrary to popular belief, but they do protect your hair from injury and discourage your hair from distracting you while you are bathing. Speedo makes great swimming hats, theirs we highly recommend!

Nose clips and earplugs can help protect your ears and avoid flooding your nose with water when you pass through the spray.

Swim paddles are another piece of equipment that, if you're an absolute beginner, can help strengthen your legs for swimming.

Kickboards are a perfect tool to have for swimming. Kicking laps up and down the pool is a great alternative when you just want to focus on your footwork and work those legs!

SWIMMING TIPS

Whether your technique or skill, or whether you're a beginner swimmer or a globally ranked competitor, the fundamentals of pool development remain the same. Here are 7 tips for swimming faster.

1. Start on your technique.

Jumping into the pool and pounding out a couple of sets at maximum intensity will give you a great workout, there's no question about it, but how much of the training is achieved with amazing technique?

It's enticing to want to base our pool success on sheer effort and will, but if you're serious about wanting to swim faster you also have to swim with intent and intention. It ensures you perform your swimming exercises with both commitment and concentration as you exercise intentionally.

A good swimmer has the absolute basis of having great technique. When you advance, poor technique serves for your skills as a glass ceiling, something that we will discuss more in a few moments.

2. Take a step at a time.

It is difficult to try to make changes to the distribution methodology and will leave you feeling exhausted. Focus on one thing at a time until you completely nail it down, and then move on to the next.

Conversely, if you have to focus entirely on various aspects of your stroke and preparation, begin by separating them by collection.

Therefore, you'd focus exclusively on maintaining a high elbow grab during your warm-up, for example. You'd be working on correct body roll during the pre-set. As both of them become consistent swimming fixtures they will mix in with your regular stroke.

Concentrate on one thing and do it nuts well in the tub.

3. Provide suggestions.

Our biases are almost without number. We exaggerate our doubts, downplay our talents, and make us think we worked harder than we might possibly have on the package. We apply also to how we interpret our methodology.

The entrance to the hand turns out not to be as big as we figured. When we get tired we lose our elbow, without realizing. And so forth.

In the case of training solo, having a coach or video feedback will help you correct errors in your technique early on.

Being swum is a lot of meters and yards ahead of you, and it's fundamental to get your stroke right before jumping into them. The further you go through your swimming career the more difficult it becomes to make adjustments and change course.

Practice, get feedback, request, and repeat.

4. Emulate specialist.

One of my favorite ways to get hyped before training is to boot some of my favorite swimmers from a pair of YouTube videos.

Whether it's Matt Biondi's floating, effortless freestyle, or watching giant underwater dolphin kicks from Phelps or Lochte's leg, watching other swimmers swim the way I want to swim makes me internalize the motions when I get into the water later.

We react to mimicry well through something in our brains called mirror neurons, which lets us internalize others ' gestures and behavior, giving credence to the phrase "monkey see, monkey do." 5. Be an output Guru.

Air puts up resistance. A whole bunch thereof. Because at sea level, swimmers are almost 800 times denser than air, they are constantly warring against water resistance.

Through streamlining, washing our heads, throwing on expensive tech costumes, we're still battling the water pressure.

Swimming is not always about being faster or slower, but rather about being more effective. When you look at the body of a swimmer, you begin to understand what I mean; they are slim formed and built to combat water depth. Michael Phelps, weighing around 190 pounds* only* at 6'4

Lean, Powerful.

Alexander Popov, arguably the greatest sprint freestyler of all time, would regularly swim long freestyle bouts, all while exploring the nooks and corners of his stroke, endlessly seeking ways to make it more efficient and easier to slide through the water.

Try to make the stroke more effective by making it slow, while keeping a low water profile as well.

6. Practice, work out, practice.

The sport's top swimmers make it look supremely simple, don't they? We can watch someone like Michael Phelps swim and say to ourselves that it must be quick, because it seems so natural.

The confident movement hides a sense of skill and relentless determination over years of training to practice better and faster. We have won the "fast" and powerful stroke in the pool over miles and miles of focused meters and yards.

Whether it's going to the Olympics or joining the varsity team at high school it requires practice.

This needs the repetitions to occur and to bring in.

Swimming for a few stretches with excellent technique and great effort is awesome; doing so for weeks, months and years is good over and over again.

7. Count, and proceed.

Swimming is a numeral sport. Stroke numbers, stroke frequencies, cycles and heart rates all add up to a dream come true for a statistician.

They give you, most critically, very concrete, observable milestones that you can focus on advancing and developing over time.

Focus on the number that most matters to you, and work to improve it.

Progression should be the ultimate goal within the pool from week to week. Progression, after all, serves as a positive IV-drip, offering a steady and consistent sense of momentum that will keep you focused and motivated to work hard at the pool.

Whether you're doing more meters at the speed of the run, pounding out more than 100 at a certain time, or keeping a certain stroke count over longer and longer lengths, there are endless ways to measure and improve your swim.

CHAPTER THREE

HOW TO TRAIN FOR YOUR FIRST ADULT SWIM LESSONS

It can be both easy and challenging for adults to learn how to swim. Although adults are more able to grasp such concepts than adolescents, they also find themselves afflicted by low confidence and confusion. Their worries of what they might look like in a swimsuit, or how stupid they might look when learning how to swim, might hold them back and keep them from giving their best shot. The best way to combat this is to learn the basics of swimming, building trust and feeling comfortable in the water.

Get the correct stuff Get the perfect bathing suit. Choose a suit that fits perfectly, is relaxed and you can step in. When you leap into the water it shouldn't come off. Skip the embellished beach or pool bikinis and baggy swim trunks; you need something that's sleek and easy to move in.

• Be extra cautious about white colour. It can be seen through when warm, depending on the padding.

Put on a swim cap. It will not only protect your hair against the chlorine, but it will also streamline your body and reduce water friction. If you have long hair, make sure first tie it up, then tuck it under the hat.

• Many bathing caps have silicone in them. If you're allergic to latex, read the label, and make sure you buy a latex-free swimming hat.

Buy good goggles which are not going to spill.

Nothing in the eyes kills a swim quicker than mud. Grab sunglasses that go over your eyes, so make sure they're at peace. Never get those which cover the mouth and nose. If possible, try on the glasses in the store before you buy–if not, make sure you get goggles with an extendable nose bridge. This will insure proper match. You may want to find prescription swim goggles, which are not much more expensive than normal sunglasses, because you usually require glasses to see. You will be able to see the coach plainly, and they can make the process of swimming more fun.

• Some are made from rubber. If you are allergic to latex, make sure to check the package before you first buy anything; it will warn you if it contains latex, or not.

Consider getting some more equipment for the pool.

Most people find that things such as pool noodles, kickboards, and flippers assist with different swimming aspects. When you suggest these things to your swim coach then you might want to consider buying them as well.

- You can also purchase nasal pads and ear plugs to prevent water from reaching your nose and ear.

- Make sure to get a sunscreen while bathing in an outdoor pool.

Learning to breathe

Comfortably put your face into the water. Make sure you have got your sunglasses on. You may need to change the goggles at this stage by tugging on the belts so they are not leaking.

- You should practice this part in a bowl of warm water if you're not feeling comfortable going into the pool yet. The pipe will inhale and exhale twice the size of your nose. Then take a deep breath through your lips, then put your face into the water. Slowly exhale through your mouth, just enough to prevent water from getting into your lungs.

• Many swimmers like to exhale through their mouth and nose. When you find this more convenient for you, then you should do it.[2]• Many swimmers find wearing a nose plug allows them to exhale smoother underwater. You should take twice as much time to breathe out as you should inhale. If this is hard to keep track of, try pacing the exhalation to the count of ten.

Relax by raising your mouth out of the water to breathe and in the water to have your nose. At some point, you'll actually get water in your mouth while you're underwater. While that may feel uncomfortable, it is not an impression of near-death. This happens to a lot of people, especially when they know how to swim first.

One way to reduce the amount of water swallowed is "Keh.

Remember to focus on the bottom of the pool. This is a good habit, even if you haven't swim yet. It helps to straighten and align your body. If you move your head away from the water, your body will tilt upwards, increasing resistance and resistance. It will be difficult to swim.

If your pool has these black lanes, use them as focus.

Confident in water

Enter the water and move your arm up and down. You will feel resisting water pressure, and you may notice it moving your body. Move your arm sideways and your body will rotate. Press down to move your body up. Move your body up. Move your arms back and your body will lean forward.

This can be standing or sitting, but you need to be in the water up to your shoulders.

This is sometimes called "skull ring".

Go to slightly deeper water where you can still stand. Make sure your head is out of the water.

Hold on to the wall and start to shake up and down. Remember to push your feet out of the pool floor and exhale through your mouth.

When you're ready, wave your hand off the wall. Push up the bottom with your feet and grab the wall. Skull and kick while standing up

Keep doing this until you feel comfortable in the water without grabbing the edge of the pool. You can move further away from the edge of the pool if necessary. Remember that it is not deeper than where you can still stand. Thus, if you lose confidence, all you have to do is get up.

Play in the water until you feel comfortable and relaxed. Get used to that your face is underwater and your body is stretched. Use buoyancy devices and try to reduce your dependence on fear of going underwater. You can also swim a little before floating. The main reactions in water are stretching on the water surface, skulls, kicks, breathing and relaxing.

If you accidentally swallow the water, do not be discouraged. It happens to everyone, even experienced swimmers.

Floating and moving learning

Develop a habit of keeping your body straight, like piercing a needle in water. If your hips are lower than your shoulders, your body will tilt up and you will not be able to stay floating. You can practice this by balancing on a bed, bench, or chair.

Please float on your back first. Keep your back between your shoulder blades and keep your body as straight as possible. Move your arms sideways, wave your hands, and lift your palms from your hips. This will help you stay floating.

Backfloating is one of the easiest ways to learn how to float.

If you have problems with this, please consult someone with swimming experience.

Roll your body slightly from side to side and breathe with your head sideways. Prone to exhale and turn over on chest and stomach. This is the position for most swimming styles, including freestyle and breaststroke.

Practice arm strokes. This can be done underwater or on a bench / chair. Put your arms behind your head, above your head, and in a circular motion.

Practice flutter kick. Grip beside the pool, pool noodles or kickboard and gently kick your feet with a soft fluttering motion. Keep your toes sharp and your feet as straight as possible. Do not kick from the knee or kick hard. This increases resistance and reduces speed.

This is the basic kick for swimming. It can be on your back or down.

The kick must be done with little effort. Increasing the kick does not always mean faster.

You can also practice kicks while balancing on the bench.

Hold the kickboard or noodle and stretch your chin into the water to kick. Go 5-10 yards (4.6-9.1 m), exposing your face to water. Do some wraps like this until you are comfortable. You can keep your face from soaking in water for the first length, but try to work out where you can swim your face under water. This allows you to practice breathing. Also, it may be easier to swim!

You can start practicing in shallow waters until you feel calm and then move on to deeper waters.

When you are confident, try without a kickboard and add arm movement.

Use a water exercise or flotation belt around your waist while improving your skills. It is a great exercise to use it after you learn to swim. This can be done while stepping on with the belt on.

You can also wear swimming fins during your kick practice. However, always wear it, especially during warm-up and warm-down exercises

Always be safe. Learning to swim is not a competition. Save it for when you become more experienced. If you do not feel comfortable at the current depth, do not force yourself to move to deeper waters. If you feel tired, take a break and get out of the deep.

Don't be discouraged by experienced swimmers around you because everyone started with the basics. They don't think about you or make fun of you. After all, they were also in your position at some point.

HOW TO THREAD WATER

Treading water is usually the first thing you learn when you start swimming lessons, and if you're ever stuck in deep water for any length of time it could be the one thing that saves your life. Water treading is a method used to keep your body and eyes above the water, so you can breathe. Conserving strength and remaining calm are key factors when you tread water...... Relax while you tread water in any situation you need to be as relaxed as possible. Anxiety can cause tension in your body, and may cause cramping or hamper your technique. Breathe deeply and steadily as long as your head is safely above the surface and you will be able to maintain your position for much longer.

SCULLING

Sculling is a technique that you use with your arms and hands to help keep your head contact with the surface. You bend your knees slightly while you are in a vertical water-treading position, and stretch your arms at shoulder level to the sides. At 45 degrees, you turn your palms to the front and at the same time, bring your arms to the front. Flip your hands forward, so when your arms are half way to the front, they are 45 degrees toward the wall. Continue to maintain pressure against the water in this fashion and keep your body near the surface.

Flutter Kick You must also move your legs while you are raising your arms in a sculling motion. The flutter kick is a useful movement of the legs for various swimming strokes, and for water treading. Essentially, it's just an alternating jump of one leg and then the next, with your feet pointing towards the bottom of the pool in quick motions. Vary the flutter kick pace when learning how to tread water, choosing the speed that works best for your body type.

Balance Your upper and lower body synchronization and balance is what really brings your head above water. You can have the most beautiful flutter kick and the most effective sculling technique, but if the moves aren't coordinated you'll sink.

Water treading is the main method of survival that allows you to keep your head above water, keeping you from falling under and eventually drowning.

Step1:Start Practice the arm movement in shallow water when standing in it. Arms are equally important for treading water as legs.

The "skulling" moment of the arm involves sweeping your forearms back and forth, moving outwards and backwards towards your body. Keep your wrists in motion and tilt your palms on the outward stroke away from your body, and on the inward stroke back towards your body. This will push the water from the force of your forearms around you.

Step 2: Switch to deeper water where the feet are unable to reach the bottom so keep hanging onto the pool side.

Keep your body upright, your hands below. Move the legs in a gesture of a scissor, known as the move of the flutter. Do not bend your knees, but keep your legs open and balanced with your toes pointed back.

Step 3: Continue. Lets go and practice the arms and legs together, staying close to the wall. At first, a floatation device can be used to help. The kick action can get quite easily boring, so it's helpful to learn the second kick move that can keep you afloat for longer.

Step 4. Practice the circular kick action, which is less painful but marginally easier to practice than the flutter jump, by hanging on to the side of the pool once more and keeping your legs directly behind you. This is an effective kick to the breaststroke.

Put your legs up straight, hitting your feet, knees and toes sticking out like a ballet dancer.

Keep your heels together and bend your knees to and fro to raise your heels to your body.

Kick your legs down and to the sides, still with your toes pointing out, as if you were standing at the bottom of the pool with your legs apart.

Bring your heels back together, in the first position of the straight leg, ready to start the cycle once more.

Continue this step while gripping the bottom of the water, until you feel at ease with the action.

Step 5: Keep a floatation device (such as a kickboard) to exercise the rotation of the legs away from the wall but still close enough to keep the wall if necessary. Put aside the floatation assist when you're ready, and incorporate the skulling of the arm movement with the circular movement legs of the breast stroke.

Each time you should be able to keep that treading water going for longer periods. Start with ten seconds, then slowly work up to one minute.

Practicing your water noodle coordination will allow you a margin of error while practicing. Wrap the noodle around the neck, so that the ends are under the axes. Do the sculling technique and the flutter kick simultaneously until you feel supported by the noodle without the assistance.

Mastered with this experience, you can increase your safety level in the water tremendously.

Finally, drop the noodle but if you need help, have a lifeguard or a strong swimmer nearby.

HOW TO RELAX IN THE WATER

Within the water your body can float. Your lungs are full of air which ultimately transforms you into a floaty toy in human form. So why do humans sink as they crash into the water? Because not calming.

If your body is calm you are going to float to the water surface. However, of course, if you fall into the water the instant reaction is panic and fear that makes relaxation really difficult. Thankfully there's a simple exercise you can do to relax in the water to get healthy. It is called The Float of the Dead Man.

Learning the Dead Man's Float

The Dead Man's Float is done on your stomach, facing the bottom of the pool while your body floats at the surface of the water surface and your back is outed to the air.

Start by standing in the pool or crouching (depending on how deep it is), with your hands on the water surface, Take a deep breath, tuck your head and put your face in the water. Lets the body relax gradually, Your hips will begin floating down to the water surface. Your legs are likely to continue to dangle and that's good.

Then shift your arms above your head in line with your torso until your hands are just below the water's surface. This should put your legs up higher to the water surface. When you relax your body rests on the surface of the water in a straighter line.

The more you do the float of the Dead Man, the better you will be in the water to calm your muscles. This will make swimming safer, because you won't have extra tension in your body and it will also make it easier to relax and stay calm if you're ever in a water emergency.

HOW TO GLIDE THROUGH THE WATER

Gliding when swimming takes place before the start of a stroke, in strokes, after a flip turn or at the end of a lap. Proper gliding method allows a swimmer to keep momentum as they brace for the next stroke. Gliding also provides good exercise to improve the core muscles of the body. Proper gliding technique can improve the overall swimming rhythm and increase the swimming stroke rate, resulting in an effective cardiovascular training.

Grasp one hand's fingers with the other hand's fingers by placing your first hand fingers on top of each other with your thumb underneath. Bend your knees and lift your feet off the pool wall, straighten your whole body in the water with your hands clasped in front and your head firmly tucked in between your shoulders. Glide until you feel sluggish in the water and take the first step of a swim.

Take a brief glide to distinguish each swim stroke. As in the case of freestyle and backstroke, when your arm enters the water over your head, holding it completely stretched for a few minutes before pulling the left hand back out of the water for the next stroke. That will keep your pace steady and increase your pool momentum.

Glide straight into the water with your torso, hands out in front, after every turn flip. Use the muscles in your legs to push firmly off the wall and straighten your body until you slowly feel the momentum; then take the next stroke.

To actually make benefits in your swimming pace, practice streamlining your glide. Holding your arms straight with your head firmly tucked between them while pointing your toes and holding your knees straight and together will help reduce lag and increase each swim stroke's consistency and effectiveness.

Use the glide exercise mid-swim to gage the stance, line and balance when swimming. Do this by completing a side-gliding spot on one of the strokes. Leave the arm that just finished pulling by your side at rest while the other arm remains stretched out in front. Your nose is still to be pointing at the bottom of the pool. See how far you can float alone on inertia before you nearly come to a complete stop before making your next stroke, without hitting. The further you float, the more smooth your position, before you need to stroke again.

HOW AND WHEN TO BREATHE

Having your nose wet feels as good as touching your funny bone or getting a piece of sand in your cheek. But if this summer you are swimming laps in a pool or ocean, and your training is somewhat rusty, you may find yourself in this predicament. Reminding yourself to breathe is hard work—especially if you're underwater.

One of the main differences between swimming and other activities is the ability to learn how to breathe under water.

One of the greatest problems for every beginner swimmer is having good breathing technique. Since breathing is instinctual, it naturally comes to us all without conscious thinking so little emphasis is placed on studying it.

In swimming it's important to have a rhythm to your breathing. Breathing problems can lead to incorrect stroke tactics such as poor body alignment and swimming on the lob-side.

There is a bit of skill involved with breathing while swimming and finding the right way to do it for your own health and pleasure is a good idea. Swimming is an outstanding low-impact aerobic exercise, which ensures your heart and lungs are functioning and your muscles are improved without damaging your joints. Once you figure out the whole thing about breathing and stroking, when you get bored with the stair climber or elliptical swimming could become your go-to workout. "Once you nail the correct breathing pattern, your swimming will improve drastically," Use your mouth.

If you try to breathe with your nose alone, you are more likely to get water from your nose. "When swimming, breathing out of your mouth is much safer and more efficient,. You must also exhale your breath beneath the water rather than attempting to inhale and exhale once your head is above water, and inhale when your head is above water. Stand by the pool wall and inhale through your mouth, then drop under water to exhale through your nose until it feels natural. Smoothly move your head.

"Whatever you do with your head while swimming, your body is going to follow," many people tend to jerk their head back and forth as they swim in an attempt to breathe out of their mouth's side. But your head must only turn to the side enough to provide a breath through your mouth and afterwards turn back and exhaling slowly through your nose While on the ground, practice switching your head side by side, looking straight past your shoulder, "Once you are relaxed with this movement, bring it into the water and training by lying face down in the water and flipping your head slowly to each side," Just let one eye rise from the water— the other half below should be below the surface.

Perform fitness exercises.

Swimming in a lap pool can be intimidating so take some extra time before you venture out to practice this skill. Start by taking a horizontal "superman" spot on the wall and turning your head side by side, "Try to keep the waterline down the center of your face when breathing in the breeze." "It prevents facing forward or backward that interferes with your body line in the pool." Instead, once that feels good, switch to using a kickboard instead of a wall, And consider if you're a novice, all this should be performed under the watchful eye of a professional swim instructor, mentor or lifeguard to optimize your ability.

Here's a look at three popular swim styles with the right breathing techniques.

Front Crawl: While swimming the front crawl, turning your head either too early or too late is a common mistake which ends up causing your body position to go out of alignment. Start turning your head when the pulling process is over. Take a quick breath as the arms recover over water and return your head to the starting position again.

Make sure you turn your head sideways and don't lift your whole head off the water. It is counterproductive to lift it out of the water, as it will cause your hips to sink, making it even harder to breathe.

Breaststroke: Plan to relax during the breaststroke when both of your arms draw against your chest. Your pectorals and muscles in the back should help your arm move to help your head out of the water. Getting the timing right is critical since breathing at the wrong time will affect your stroke.

Butterfly: Your arms should pull hard down in the butterfly to propel your body for a breath above the water. At the end of the pulling phase, it is essential to start getting out of the water. Upon moving your head back to the starting point again as your muscles heal, your mouth should be free of the water surface for a short breath.

Quick tips to help improve your breathing techniques:

- Calm-Make sure your facial muscles are not tensed despite inadequate transmission of air results.
- Breathe Out-Instead of breathing out when swimming, most novice swimmers tend to hold their breath underwater. You should breathe out softly while your face is immersed in water so bubbles will fly out of your mouth or nose.
- Breathe In-The bulk of swimmers breathe in their ears. This action should be quick, and only last a second.
- Timing-Breathing out in the water should be about twice as long as you breathe in over the surface as it helps to build a relaxed breathing pattern.

HOW TO SWIM FREESTYLE

Freestyle is the world's most popular swimming movement, and it's an essential skill that every swimmer can work on. They truly believe that each individual swimmer has at least one aspect of their freestyle stroke that can be enhanced and perfected.

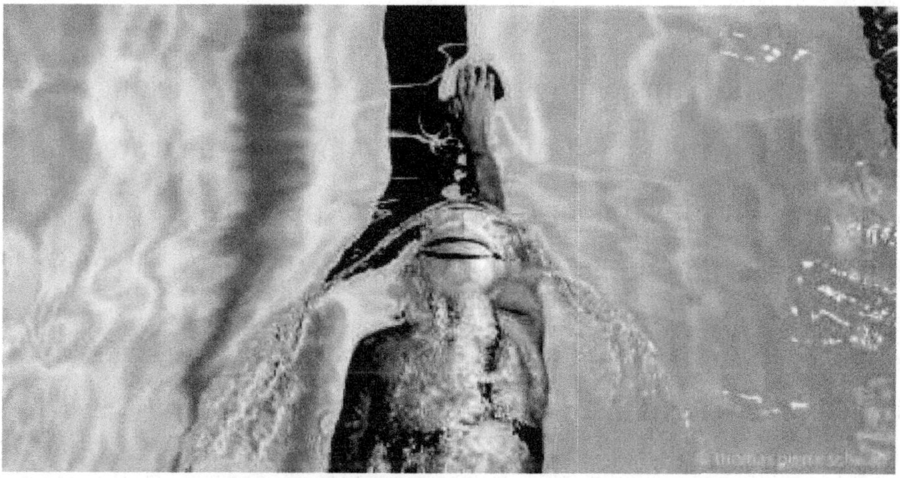

1–Streamline body positioning: The most important part of swimming is streamline concept. This is when your body is as thin as possible, going through the water so you can reduce the drag.

Head Position

The location of your head is important, and where your eyes look. Try looking down as you swim freestyle, and keep your attention on the bottom of the pool. You should have your neck and head in a neutral position, right over your shoulders. You shouldn't have your head or legs lifted up before you. Keeping your feet fixed on the bottom of the pool holds your legs higher in the water, making jumping in the water safer.

Hip Position With your eyes focused on a neutral head position, your hips will naturally lift up, making kicking a lot easier. Try focusing your upper body down in the water, making your hips higher in the water, Apply fast, strong flutter kicks and the legs will be right on the water surface.

2–Catch The "catch" refers to pulling water in your arms as your body moves forward.

Fingertips The hands should be in a tight cupping position, with the fingers pressed against each other to prevent water from sliding through. Cup your hands in a place which might hold some water in your palm. You shouldn't be perfectly flat but also not bent, or else your palms won't float in the water as easily.

Your fingertips will enter the water at an inclination of 45 degrees towards the surface about 12-18 inches in front of your head. Your middle finger should first enter the water, followed by a sustained stretch through your arm and shoulder. When your shoulder is fully extended, your shoulders should fall to the left, keeping your head facing downward. This is the start of your catch, where you'll start pulling water with your full arm.

EVF

EVF reflects an Early Vertical Forearm. You must stretch your hands toward the bottom of the pool after your arm is fully extended out, trying to keep your forearm as straight as possible so it serves as a sail, dragging a lot of water behind you as a propeller on the surface.

Pull Step You should begin your pull after your arm bends down at the elbow. You're going to want to draw straight down to your body's edge, holding your hand cupped until your elbow hits your thighs. Try not to cross your arms along the center of your body, as you want to directly focus your momentum.

3–Rotation Shoulders & Shoulders You will want to keep your head in place every time you take a stroke, and use your shoulders to move to the right and left. The action will be started by your hands, and accompany your arms. Instead of starting with shoulder flips, try to focus on turning the body with your heart Pairing these two parts of your body should keep your body in a perfect position for streamlining along the water surface.

4–Breathing head position & rotation: Having a balanced head position is the most important part of the breathing in your freestyle move. You want to move your head forward or backwards now as this will wreck your body position and consume more time than you need.

You will take a stroke of one arm while breathing and you will find your entire upper body moving to the left when you step out. Your head and neck will follow the same movement, and move when raising your mouth. You'll move your head and neck together to your side, hold one eye underwater and open your mouth to breathe. When you turn, the water line should be right in the middle of your nose.

Make sure to focus on your opposite arm, as it should be extended out in front of you toward the water surface. This extension will keep your body more balanced and allow you to push forward with the momentum. If you pull down your arm while breathing it will stop you moving forward.

5–Kicking Keep It Simple The most common problem faced by beginners is kicking too much and getting too big. This is an easy way to ruin and actually slow your body positioning. We recommend that you keep it simple, and de-emphasize your kick. For beginners–your body positioning, breathing, and arms are going to be much more important and the kick should be an afterthought focused on just rotating your body.

Short & Fast Kicks From The Hips You'll be using a flutter kick in freestyle. Try to keep your legs nearly straight, with a gentle hop that travels only from the knees to your feet. Out of your thighs comes power and strength. As you move through the water your legs are supposed to kick in a short and fast motion. Try not to over-bend your knees. Bigger kicks, taller than 12 inches in height, would take up too much space and kill your spot on streamline.

6–Silent Heading, Touching, Smelling, Degusting and Seeing Focus on all your senses as you move through the water, such intense focus and thoughtfulness will help you to refine your stroke and pinpoint where in the water you may not be as successful. The goal is to make the least amount of noise when you float, which ensures you move in a smooth motion through the mud.

And above all, being conscious of your water experience will make your swimming much more enjoyableIt's a great opportunity to connect with your body, mind and spirit and just relax in the pool. We always recommend a few laps of silent swimming to end any exercise!

CHAPTER FOUR

LEARNING TO GO UNDER WATER

Underwater diving is a talent best achieved with relaxation. A great place to start for beginners is breath keeping exercises and drenching exercises.

The more comfortable you are in the water, the less oxygen our body uses, and then the greater the amount of time spent underwater.

Perhaps one of the most important stages in learning to swim is the ability to submerge the face, especially when overcoming a fear of water.

Some beginners arrive with that built-in ability and need only be taught how to breathe while swimming. It will be one of the most terrifying tasks for others that you face.

Three Stages to Swim Underwater 3 key steps are required to work through to become confident in submerging underwater. To beginners or those with a fear of water these are important. Others find it easy. The three phases are:

- Wet face
- Breathing and partly submerging

- Full submersion and underwater swimming It goes without saying that a careful approach is needed here.

One stage at a time, and you move to the next level only when you are happy and confident.

Stage 1: Getting the face wet Remember: getting the face wet and being splashed into the face are two completely different concepts, each with different effects and not always positive ones. Here are some activities to go through: blowing bubbles on the surface of the water, or spinning an obstacle while you float underwater. You can either softly blast "like blowing through a pipe" or violently blow "like blowing candles on a cake"

Split water into your own mouth, and put it on your forehead.

Throwing and catching a ball provides an outstanding diversion from the water splashes. If the ball is designed to drop just in front of you, because of the pressure of catching the ball this will end in a wet face without too much thought. The smallest of splashes from the softest throws is enough to have a positive effect.

Step 2: Partially submerge the face You need to learn how to hold your breath by "breathing in and holding everything in."

Some will be able to do this effortlessly, others will know through trial and error when you submerge your face partly and discover that you can't breathe underwater!

An object can then be placed just below the surface of the water, shallow enough to see and reach for it, but deep enough to submerge the mouth in order to reach it. Once confidence is gained with this exercise, then the object can be slightly lowered to encourage a submergence of the mouth and nose.

These practices are best executed in the water with an assistant holding the object for you. This may also help to boost your trust with someone in the water with you.

Step 3: Complete Submersion and Swimming Underwater

Stage 2 naturally leads quickly to step 3 where the target is put below the surface of the water where you are helped to recover it by submerging your head completely underwater. Breath holding should be more accomplished by this stage and you should start relaxing more as you immerse yourself. Swimming underwater finally becomes a natural development.

Progression from this point is to integrate face submerging, either partially or completely, when swimming different strokes and even retrieving artifacts across lengths or widths from the pool deck.

All of the above steps help the process of learning how to swim underwater tremendously. It's important to understand your own buoyancy, as this can be a crucial factor that can determine how safe it is to swim underwater. If your body has strong buoyancy then it is more difficult to submerge underwater and float, though not impossible.

BASIC FLOATING EXERCISE

Everyone can learn how to float in water, and should. Knowing how to float can save your life, and it's the first step in learning freestyle swimming. It may seem daunting, or absolutely impossible, but the first thing you need to do is believe you can float.

Finding a Trainer is the next step. If you are afraid of the water, they will give you the courage to conquer your initial concerns and help you to relax in the water while in healthy surroundings. Your body's flotation features Let's begin with a basic physics principle: anything that has a higher density than water will sink in water.

The human body is about two-thirds fat, by weight. This means that your density resembles that of water. And you shouldn't have to do much effort, if any, to float on top of the water. That being said, your body composition may affect your ability to float naturally.

Men tend to have more muscle density than women, in general terms. People with higher muscle density, or very slender muscle (a very low fat-to-muscle fiber ratio), will tend to sink more. So, if you're young, a man, or a very athletic woman, good mechanics and technique will be of great assistance to you. Yet your body still wants more of a float than it wants to sink.

Your lung capacity can also make a difference in the ease with which you can stay on top of the water. People with higher lung capacity are going to float a little more easily, for two reasons. Secondly, they have in their chest a bigger pocket of air.

Then, second, they appear to carry more blood in their bodies. Oxygen is less dense than water, so the more oxygen you have in your body, the more you are going to be buoyant. Now that you know why your body may be more or less inclined to float, here are three ways in which you can improve how you float in water.

Relax: The key to floating is for beginners ironically a big challenge: you have to relax. You will be able to "swim" as long as you learn that. Train in shallow water until you have faith in your natural ability to float and get your face used to being in the water since this is another aspect that can contribute to your fears. Note the breathing pattern if you can float but you're still stressed.

Not only is deep breathing medically proven to help your body relax, it will also add more oxygen to your lungs which should make you more breathable. Look at the sky (or the ceiling if inside), and breathe in deeply. At each breath fill your lungs with oxygen–feel the air traveling all the way down to the lower end of your lungs (near the bottom of your rib cage).

Hold your breath for a brief moment, and feel atop the water essentially weightless. Exhale and then repeat. Improve Your Float Mechanics Relax slowly back into the water allowing you to recline your shoulders and head as if lying in bed. Small hand gestures would allow you to stay face-up out of the water with your mouth and nose, and to start breathing naturally. You can either raise your hands above your head or lift off slightly from the floor, if your legs still fall.

You are building a wider pillar above your knees by raising your arms above your head, which gives you more leverage to raise your legs up to the surface. It will bring your legs higher up in water at the very least. Strengthen your technique Get your abdominal muscles involved.

Use your core force to lift your body towards the surface. You might conceive of a string attached to your belly button, which lifts your body to the top of the water. The bond is strong between your mind and your body. If you can just imagine the string pulling your belly and feet to the water's surface, your muscles will probably be organizing themselves and making it happen! Gently kick. Kick. Don't kick too hard you've got a push forwards. But it will help to bring them to the surface and keep you calm, very soft and gentle, alternating leg movements. Of course stay relaxed as you do this.

Methodical small motions with your hands and feet will help to keep you stabilized and close to the water surface. If you don't move your legs you'll notice they're inclined to sink downwards. Enjoy Weightlessness Once you relax and float on your back, take a moment to enjoy the feeling of holding up the water and relieving the pressure from your joints and muscles. You can use a pool noodle to help support you under your shoulders or knees for extended floating time periods. These should be used as floating aids and not competently relied on to keep you afloat.

Steps to stay afloat while you swim...

Exercise 1:

Face Down Floating

Learn how to float in the water Take a deep breath and submerge your face up to the surface. Lay face down to cover as much surface area as possible with the arms and legs broad. Lay there in this relaxed position as long as you can hold your breath and hear how your body is doing.

First you will most likely find your legs sinking slowly. See if there are any small moves that can slow down their sinking rate or even help them to return to the surface.

Try a very slow breaststroke, and feel your way through the water.

Exercise 2: Push and glide

Push and glide to help prevent water sinking Take a deep breath away from the pool wall, face down. Verify that your body is in a relaxed, smooth position. Glide in one step, as far as you can.

You can find that as the momentum slows, you start sinking. See what tiny movements of the legs, feet and hands can keep you moving and floating.

Feel your way through the water with a soft move of breaststroke or front crawl.

Exercise 3: Push and Glide With Kicking

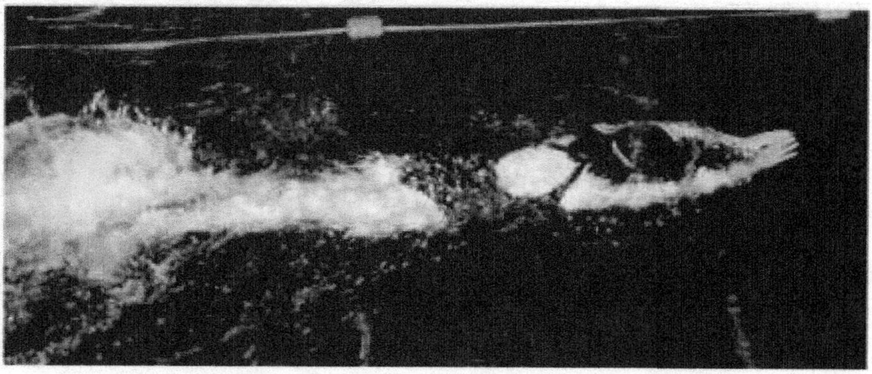

Push and Kick to help stay on the surface of the water: The same exercise with push and glide from the poolside as #2.

Add leg kicks this time to help keep the momentum going and to prevent sinking. Use a leg kick in the front crawl or type of breaststroke.

Exercise 4: Supine Push and Glide

Push and glide in a supine (face up) position on the back face up position Push and glide from the poolside. Make sure the head looks upwards, and the shoulders and thighs are high up at the surface of the water. This will help allow your feet and legs to be on or near the surface of the water, too.

As the glide starts slipping, add a soft leg kick and hand step to hold the glide moving.

STANDING UP MID SWIM

Standing Up Mid Swim Breaststroke is the best way to learn as an adult, so having to stop and stand up halfway, particularly when you get exhausted, is one of the most important bases for swimming.

Standing from a prone position (face-down) or even a head up and facing forward position allows arms and legs to be shifted simultaneously. The shoulders pull down deep into the sea, almost to the feet, while at the same time pulling your legs forward and upward. The body is almost in a seated position just before you place the feet on the floor of the tub. If you are familiar with performing a' crunch' in the gym (laying on your back and putting your knees to your chest to work your abdominal muscles), this movement is much like that but in a more upright position.

Unable to draw the feet forward and then arch the back in an attempt to stand is the most common error. It is also very common mistake not to pull down with the hands and arms, offering a sensation of sliding down.

The standing up strategy can sometimes be more challenging as you try to keep your head above the water. It can sometimes be easier to put your face in the water and execute the partially submerged procedure, and as you get used to it you will eventually be able to do it without making your face wet.

However you do that, when it comes to standing up there are no points for style and technique so it doesn't really matter how you do it!

Standing up in the swimming pool after swimming is one of the most significant and least learned aspects of swimming instruction, when you know that you can pause and stand up when swimming, so the overall swimming style can immediately become more confident when you swim confidently in the confidence that you can stop and stand up safely whenever you need to.

Standing in the water demands that the arms and legs be shifted simultaneously. Your hands have to move directly down from a prone (face-down) stance at the same time as lowering your knees and pulling them up under your chest. The trick then is to say you're going to sit on a chair that's behind you.

Bending the knees below you will then allow your body to almost sit up and it is at that stage that you can place your feet on the floor of the water. Encouraging your body to a spot upright makes it much easier to put your feet on the pool deck.

The most common errors occur as swimmers try to stand up by arching the back without raising the legs or bending the knees. The consequence is a struggle with your legs when they try to get to the bottom of the water.

It is easier to stand from the breaststroke than from the front crawl, as both arms are needed to help stand up and the breaststroke requires both arms at the same time. Normally only one arm is out in front at any moment from the front crawl, so at the stage where you need to stand up you can put out both arms in front so that both can help pull your knees up.

Below is a clear and simple example of how to stand up for mid-swim.

FRONT CRAWL

The Freestyle, in reality, is not a stroke but a swimming competition type. The front crawl is the most common and popular stroke in freestyle events, since this form is the fastest. The term freestyle is often used as a synonym for front crawl, for this reason.

The front crawl requires that you kick your feet fluttering while reaching forward with alternating strokes. Follow these 4 steps to learn how to swim and improve the technique of swimming the forehead crawl.

Stage 1: Body position Keep your body level, with your body in line with the water surface, lying faced down in the water

Step 2: Arm Motion Only two movements-the Pull and Recovery-can break down the arm movement to the simplest form.

Push-With your hands facing down, push in-line all the way to the side of your upper thigh with a slightly bent elbow. Advanced swimmers are able to do an S-pull that maximizes the pulling process.

Recovery-Lift one arm out of the water with a bent elbow, with your hand close to your upper thigh, Rise up with a bent elbow over the water and enter the water with your finger tips.

These two motions should rotate between both hands and be shifting simultaneously.

Swimming freestyle arm movement

Step 3: Respiratory technique: Choosing a side to relax relies on the right or left hand. Turn your head sideways for a short breath (one second) as your hand is early in the recovery phase. The trick is to have your head roll with your arm movement timed.

A very common error is to lift your head upwards rather than flipping it sideways to prevent drinking water. This is actually counter-productive since it disrupts the orientation of your body and encourages you to dive further into the water.

Stage 4: Leg movement With relaxed and stable knees, point the toes behind you and jump up and down from your thighs in a continuous motion. Running off the calves isn't as successful and a simple way to remedy this is to make sure that your legs are straightened when running. Refer to the exercises you can do in the pool for more details on this to improve your swimming.

Coordination notes: The arms and legs should travel in loops together A breath should be taken on one hand with each movement of that arm A breath is taken when that arm is gone. Exhale Positive Techniques Stretch the limbs as far as they can go to allow a faster stroke as the same arms enter the water. A broad arm stroke is important for swimming speed and efficiency Maintain a good body to reduce drag and make swimming simpler

CONCLUSION

As with most other forms of exercise, getting started is the key to getting stronger. This takes time, persistence and the desire to learn the basics to improve strength and proper technique. Failure to learn the basics can make it harder to swim than necessary-but don't worry. Only take things one step at a time and you're confident you'll get it hanging up!

Start with water treading, and get comfortable in the water.

Try some laps with the kickboard, and get comfortable.

Master respiratory techniques with the kickboard (probably the most challenging part of swimming) Breathing in the water is unlike breathing on land. You need to be comfortable with your face in the water while swimming and develop a rhythm for you to breathe. You breathe out into the water with your nose and inhale and relax as you turn your head or raise up your head (depending on the stroke).

Know what strokes are.

You should start with a noodle or kickboard in the shallow end of the pool doing some doggie paddling while practicing proper breathing (exhaling under water and inhaling over water). Either by paying for some swim lessons or by using our old friend YouTube when you have questions, move to basic strokes and fine-tune your swimming moves.

Sports Workouts If you're new to swimming, you'll want to be comfortable moving around in the sports before going on 20 laps to do the butterfly stroke. Start by simply walking around in the water or hanging your legs onto the edge of the pool. Learn to tread water without help. Frog-kicking and moving your arms rhythmically, are the most effective way of staying afloat. Try to run through the water while maintaining good posture (do not lean forward) and you'll experience how water acts as a resistance. Check out our exercise on Splash & Tune Water!

When you feel comfortable in water, you're going to want to start trying out some simple movements for a lap or two and focus your personal workout regimen on how your body feels when swimming and adjust it as the stamina increases.

If you aren't sure how to organize your own workout, resources are available to help you build one. One of the best-loved beginner fitness programs in Six Weeks is the Zero to 1650 schedule that teaches you to swim a full mile (a swimmer's mile is 1650. It's the equivalent of 1,500 meters) three days a week through exercise. The progression-based strategy starts easily enough, and the challenge grows slowly. There are also apps to help with the iOS and Android.

Try adding fast drills to your lap routine if you don't want to stick to a lengthy schedule. Try to do as fast as you can some short laps with a short recovery time. Try to go faster than your normal speed just for a less intense workout. There are a number of useful swim videos out there that will help make the workouts more effective while improving the quality.

Different swimming strokes Learning a few of the main strokes is helpful before you start your water workouts. - stroke operates in different muscle classes, so the strokes you use shift to customize your exercise and target different areas.

The easiest to master are some of the most popular strokes: Freestyle or Front Crawl: the basic stroke you're on your stomach while kicking and swimming arm-over-arm.

Backstroke: You kick whilst rotating your arms on your back.

Breaststroke: It looks similar to what a dolphin does, using large arms and leg motions when shifting the head in and out of the water.

Titolo | Swimming Lessons
Autore | Miriam Fast
ISBN | 979-12-20361-05-7

Youcanprint
Via Marco Biagi 6 - 73100 Lecce
www.youcanprint.it
info@youcanprint.it

Youcanprint
Finito di stampare nel mese di ottobre 2021